INSIGHTS

BUGS, BEETLES,
AND OTHER INSECTS

JOHN FELTWELL

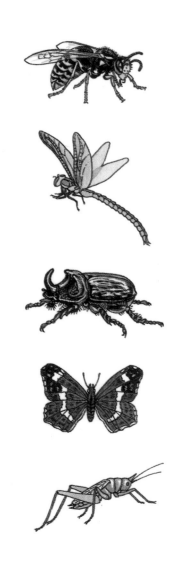

INSIGHTS

BUGS, BEETLES,
AND OTHER INSECTS

JOHN FELTWELL

Oxford University Press

A QUARTO BOOK

Published by
Oxford University Press, Walton Street, Oxford, OX2 6DP
Oxford New York Toronto Delhi Bombay Calcutta Madras Karachi
Petaling Jaya Singapore Hong Kong Tokyo Nairobi Dar Es Salaam Cape Town

and associated companies in Berlin Ibadan

Oxford is a trade mark of Oxford University Press

A catalogue record for this book is available from the British Library.

ISBN 0 19 910038 1

This book was designed and produced by
Quarto Publishing plc
The Old Brewery
6 Blundell Street
London N7 9BH

Series Consultant (Natural History) Steve Parker

Art Director Nick Buzzard
Publishing Director Janet Slingsby

Picture Manager Sarah Risley

Editor Paul Szuscikiewicz
Copy Editor Susan Berry
Designer John Grain
Design Assistant Trish Going
Illustrators Caroline Barnard, Richard Coombes, Sally Townsend

The Publishers would like to thank the following for their help in the
preparation of this book: Dave Kemp, George Keyes, Jane Molineaux,
Jane Parker, Katie Preston.

Quarto Publishing would like to thank K. G. Preston-Mafham and
R. A. Preston-Mafham – Premaphotos Wildlife – for supplying all the pictures
for this book.

While every effort has been made to trace and acknowledge all copyright
holders, we would like to apologize should any omissions have been made.

Typeset by Central Southern Typesetters, Eastbourne, East Sussex
Manufactured in Hong Kong by Regent Publishing Services Ltd
Printed in Hong Kong by Leefung-Asco Printers Ltd

Contents

WHAT ARE INSECTS? **10**   **36** FRESHWATER INSECTS

THE INSECT BODY **14**   **38** THE DRY REGIONS

FLIGHT **16**   **40** THE TEEMING RAINFORESTS

JUMPERS **20**   **42** FROM CRADLE TO GRAVE

SENSES **22**   **46** HELPFUL INSECTS

FEEDING **24**   **48** HARMFUL INSECTS

HUNTERS **26**   **50** INSECTS IN DANGER

INSECT PROTECTION **28**   **52** INSECT ESSENTIALS

INSECT HOMES **32**   **54** GLOSSARY

56 INDEX

WHAT ARE INSECTS?

Southern hawker dragonfly

Imagine you were trying to make a list of every single kind of animal in the world. When you reached the end, your list would contain one and a half million names and one million of them would be insects. There are more insects than any other kind of animal in the world, and there are more kinds of bugs and beetles than any other kind of insect. Scientists think there may be millions more insects to be discovered.

▼ **Fighter pilots**
Dragonflies belong to one of the 28 or so insect groups. You can often see them around ponds in summer and autumn. They are very good at catching other flying insects.

Black ant

Painted lady butterfly

Caddis fly

Around the edge of these two pages is a selection of some of the world's insects. Scientists have divided the insects into several groups, in order to help them with their studies. The groups are based on how closely different kinds, or species, of insect are related to one another. The pictures show insects from different groups. They are in the order of how long the group has existed on Earth. Starting with the dragonfly on the top right of this page, you can follow clockwise round the page to the black ant on the top left of this page. In doing so you are tracing the development of insect groups on the Earth. But remember that none of these pictures is life size. See if you can guess what they all have in common, and then check your answer on page 14.

Insects are so numerous because they are small and because they reproduce very quickly. Also, they are well camouflaged and are good at evading predators. So far over one million kinds – or species – of insects have been discovered by scientists. (But there are many more still waiting to be discovered.) Their tough, small bodies are made up of three

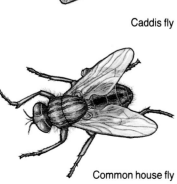
Common house fly

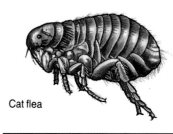
Cat flea

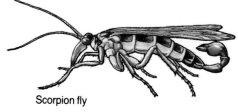
Scorpion fly

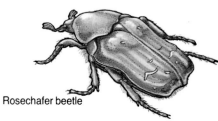
Rosechafer beetle

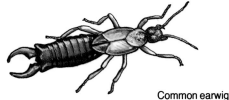
Common earwig

Soldier termite

Praying mantis

Stick insect

House cricket

Grasshopper

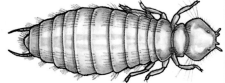
Biting louse

Thrip

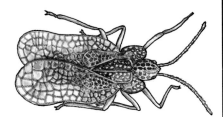
Lacebug

main parts, and their limbs have joints like your knee or elbow, although they work differently. They all wear their skeleton on the outside, unlike you or me with our bones inside.

You can think of any place on Earth, and you can bet that insects live there. They can be found on all the continents and in every kind of setting apart

▲ **In short supply**
Although the swallowtail butterfly can be found in many different places in Europe, it is uncommon where people have drained its preferred surroundings – wet marshlands – to use for farms or land for buildings. Its name comes from its hind wings.

Brown lacewing

Common alder fly

Cicada

from the sea: deserts, woods, rainforests, and even near the North and South poles.

Insects live in all sorts of strange places, but most of them can be found in what is called leaf litter – in the broken bits of last year's leaves that have got mixed up with the soil. Because you get lots of it in woodlands and at the bottom of hedgerows, you find a number of different insects in these habitats. The leaf litter not only gives them food but allows them to hide from birds and small animals that are waiting to gobble them up. Among the insects you

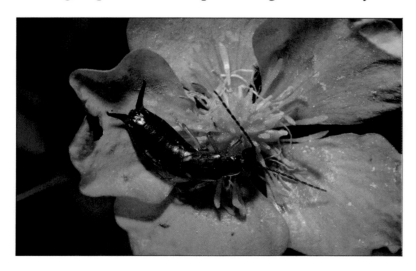

▲ **Early insect**
The earwig is one of the oldest types of insect that exists.

THE BIG FREEZE

Insects can survive in freezing conditions in the Arctic and have adapted specially to these conditions. Butterflies, for example, do not freeze because they have a special liquid in their blood which is a bit like the antifreeze used in a car's radiator to stop it freezing up in winter. In very cold conditions it takes longer for a butterfly to develop to adulthood.

▲ The common blue butterfly can be found flying in meadows north of the Arctic Circle.

▼ The dark green fritillary is found in northern Scandinavia. You can't see the dark green underside of its wings here because they are open.

WHEN IS A BUG NOT A BUG?

Sometimes a creature that looks like an insect is not at all it appears to be. Woodlice, for example, do not belong to the insect group. They are more closely related to crabs and prawns. If your house is at all damp, you will probably find woodlice in it, since they enjoy those conditions.

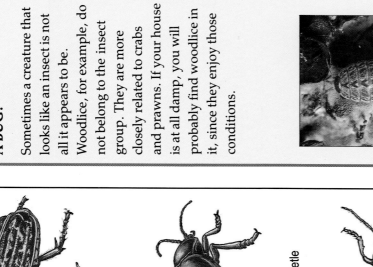

Who's in the picture?

These ten insects all appear in the picture across the bottom of these pages. Can you spot them all? You should also be able to find a column of red ants.

Pine chafer

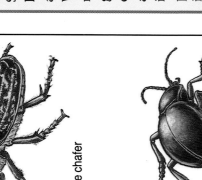
Bloody-nosed beetle

Dromius quadrimaculatus

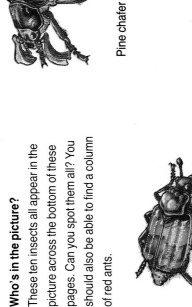
Sexton beetle

Searcher beetle

Field cricket

Violet ground beetle

Bow-winged grasshopper

Red assassin bug

Earwig

HOUSE PESTS

If you looked around your house carefully, you would find that it is home to many insects. Beetles come marching in through open doors looking for food, while other insects fly in. Moths and beetles enjoy eating your carpets. Flies and mosquitoes prefer dark rooms to the bright outdoor light. Many house insects are seen as pests, such as bed bugs and fleas.

▼ Silverfish are harmless insects which have a flattened, fish-like body.

▼ Cockroaches are found in many different buildings. They crawl around after dark, eating the food we eat, especially anything sweet. They normally live in cracks and crevices.

would find in these kinds of places are springtails, beetles, and earwigs.

Surprise, surprise!

If you look under any rock in the garden, you will be surprised to see how many insects lurk beneath it. If you turn it over really quickly, you may just be lucky enough to catch, say, a rare beetle scurrying away. All the creatures under the rock prefer to live in the dark, and a sudden flood of bright light will make them run for cover. There are plenty of other non-insect creatures such as slugs and snails which are not so quick off the mark. Earthworms move a bit faster, but if you are fortunate enough to find an ant's nest underneath the stone, you can watch for minutes as they scurry around carrying eggs and grubs to safety. Sometimes when you turn over a rock, you will come across a caterpillar, which then promptly fakes death by rolling into a ball to protect itself from attack.

▼ Insects at home
This is the floor of a typical southern European pine forest. The weather in summer is normally warm and dry, and it never gets very cold in winter. In this pleasant, mild climate you'll find all kinds of animals at home, including many kinds, or species, of insect – some of them even under stones.

THE INSECT BODY

You can identify an insect easily. Its body has three parts. The front is the head, the middle section is the thorax, and the back section is the abdomen. The head has feelers, eyes, and the mouthparts. The thorax has three pairs of legs and (in most) the wings. The insect's stomach is always in the abdomen. Yet although these features are common to all insects, they are slightly different in the different kinds of insects.

▲ Jagged edges
Many beetles, such as this longhorn from South Africa, have huge jaws for crunching up prey. The jaws are jagged like a bread knife.

▼ Breathing holes
The tiny holes in the side of this French bush cricket are used by the insect to breathe through. They are called spiracles.

▼ Inside a bee
The fully-grown insect, such as this honeybee, is more like a machine than a person – all its actions are programmed, the way a computer is. It is possible to know in advance everything an insect is about to do, because it always does the same thing in the same situation. Inside the insect there are different parts of the body, each with a special task to carry out. Some, such as the gut, are used to digest the food it eats. Others, such as the heart, are used to pump blood around the body. The brain and the nerve cord control the automatic responses.

Abdomen

Wings

Thorax

Leg

Antenna

Mouthparts

Head

Compound eye

READY, STEADY, GO

A beetle gets ready to fly. It has to get its delicate wings out from under the hard, protective wing cases.

▼ The wings are much larger than the cases and are folded up beneath them.

▲ As the wing cases are raised, the wings unfold.

▲ Take-off – flapping its hind wings, the beetle pushes itself into the air with its legs.

◀ Takeoff

The cardinal beetle lifts off with its heavy protective wing cases held high and out of the way. They are used to help the beetle balance during flight, and to protect the beetle's hind wings and body when the beetle is at rest. It is also thought that they provide aerodynamic lift in the same way that an aeroplane's wings do.

These wing cases are called elytra. Many insects still have two pairs of wings, but in beetles the front pair have adapted to form this protective case.

▲ Holding pattern

Instead of flying in a specific direction, some insects can hover like a helicopter. This male robberfly hovers over a leaf in the rainforests of Costa Rica.

▼ Sealed case

Not every beetle can still fly. The wings of this Dorcadron scopoli beetle are locked away forever. Its wing case has fused shut permanently.

The legs of all insects are similar. Each part is hinged together like the joints in a suit of armour, and at the end of the leg they always have two single claws.

Wings and mouths

Insect wings are very thin, and you can almost see through a lot of them. They also have several veins that make them stiff enough to use for flying.

There are three different kinds of insect mouthparts. Some, including all bugs, have a long snout or "beak" that pierces the food they want to eat. Others, such as all beetles, have jaws that move from side to side. A third kind has a sort of sponge that absorbs liquid.

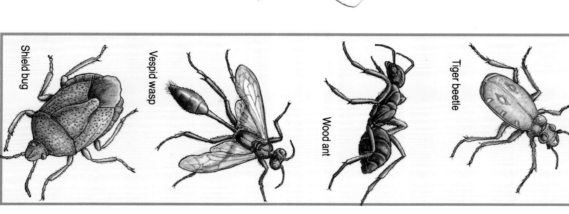

Brain

Foregut

Midgut

Heart

Hindgut

Muscles

Nerve cord

Air sacs

Tracheal openings

Ovary

▲ No beauty
The heads of crickets and grasshoppers are mainly taken up with their large jaws for eating plants and large eyes for seeing.

DIFFERENT SHAPES

Insects come in a variety of shapes although they all have the same basic characteristics. The abdomen of an insect could be long and thin or wide and flat. Or all three parts could be about the same size. Or they might be hard to see at all!

Tiger beetle

Wood ant

Vespid wasp

Shield bug

FLIGHT

Although there are millions of winged insects, there are plenty of others that have no use for wings. Insects that live in or on their source of food, such as fleas, lice, and bed bugs, do not need wings, but the vast majority do in order to fly around to find food, escape attack, and move to different breeding places. Sometimes the brightly-coloured wings of an insect carry a coded message: "I am very poisonous – go away."

Some insects, such as ants and termites, grow wings for a specific purpose – for example, when they want to set up a new home some distance from the original one. Once they have arrived at the new location, the wings drop off.

Winged or not?

Most winged insects do not have this ability and are stuck with the pair, or pairs, of wings they have. The cockchafer beetle, for example, as with all other beetles and earwigs, has two pairs of wings. The front pair acts as a tough shell to protect the back or hind wings when not in use, and the hind

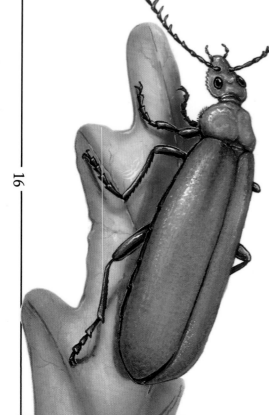

wings do all the work when the insect is in flight. It takes a lot of energy for an insect to fly, since it has to flap its wings very fast to stay airborne, but fortunately insects have super muscles that are capable of a lot of hard work. Different insects have various "flap" rates. The high-pitched whine a mosquito makes is caused by its wings pumping up and down at a thousand beats a second. Houseflies flap their wings at about 300 times a second, and the honey bee at 190 a second, while a cabbage white butterfly does a leisurely 9 beats a second. If danger looms, the flap rate can increase dramatically.

Rowing air

In each wing-beat cycle, there is an upstroke and a downstroke. The downstroke is the power stroke, which pushes the air away rather like an oar pushes through the water. As the insect moves forward, air rushes under the wings and provides lift. A butterfly can glide over several yards, using its large wings to stay airborne, but only for a limited period otherwise gravity would force it to the ground.

UP . . . AND DOWN . . .

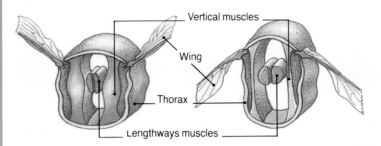

▲ The insect's thorax (the middle part of the body) from which the wings emerge is a power house of strong muscles, going from top to bottom or front to back.

The upstroke of a wing beat occurs when the vertical muscles contract and the downstroke occurs when they relax and the lengthways muscles contract.

◄ **Strong fliers**
Dragonflies and damselflies are both very powerful fliers. They beat their wings about 20 times a second. Dragonflies can also glide for short periods. As part of their courtship rituals, or to defend themselves, they rustle their wings.

▲ **Undercarriage problems**
Rather like the wheels on a plane, the insect's legs can get in the way when flying. In this empid fly, the legs are slung well below the body and out of the way of the flight movements of the wings.

Butterflies use their wings for advertisement and disguise, as well as for flight. These insects come in two types of colour: bright ones that they want their enemies to see and dull ones which they hope enemies will not. Brightly coloured insects are generally poisonous, and enemies have to learn that a bright colour means danger. Dull-coloured insects are often tasty, if only the birds could find them.

Falling scales

Hundreds of scales provide the colour on the wings of butterflies and moths. Every time they beat their wings some of the scales come off, particularly when they clap their wings together when they bring them up above their heads. Imagine how many scales a butterfly loses after beating its wings for up to ten beats a second for a couple of hours.

▲ Case for defence
The brightly-coloured wing cases of the longhorn beetle from the rainforests of South Africa protect the insect's wings and abdomen.

The wings are kept beneath it when not in use, protected from accidental damage that might be caused by bumping into things as the beetles look for food.

LOVE DUST

Some of the special scales on butterflies' wings carry powerful smells. In the male the smells are usually carried on the front wings. When a male and female butterfly are getting ready to mate with one another, they spend a lot of time fluttering around each other. When the male is very close to the female, he dusts a few of these scent scales – or "love dust" – over her in an action designed to make her want to mate.

DIRECTION FINDERS

Honey bees remember the way to flowers and other food sources by figuring out the angle between the entrance of the hive, the position of the sun, and the location of the flower. The bees are even smart enough to know how to change the angle as the sun moves through the sky during the day. It is thought that night-flying insects, like most moths, use the light of the moon to navigate. They keep it at a constant angle to their eyes. Other bright lights confuse them and they end up circling around and around.

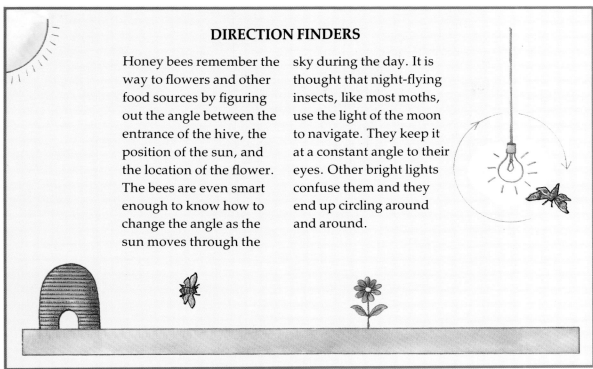

FLIGHT PATTERNS

The butterfly (top) seems to wander without purpose, although it is trying to find the scent of food or a mate. The bee (middle) flies in ever-smaller circles around its hive. The cicada (bottom) belts around as if it isn't looking where it's going.

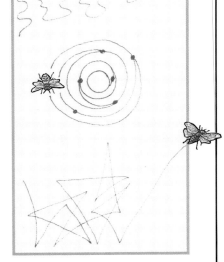

Insect navigators

As insects fly around, they have to find their way about. Bees can make use of the sun in a very clever way (see the box above). Other insects, such as the cicada, do not seem to care what way they go.

Some of the moths that are active at night always seem to be attracted by the light. They often fly right into a hot light bulb, burning their wings and plummeting to the ground.

Long distance fliers

Many animals make long journeys, or migrations, in search of food, warmth and good places to breed. The Monarch butterfly travels south from the top of North America to winter in California and Mexico. This journey may involve flying as far as 110 km (68 miles) in one day and a distance of 3,200 km (2,000 miles) over all. Imagine that with a 100 mm (4 in) wingspan!

▼ Long flier

The cockchafer is also called a maybug because it comes out of its underground cell in the spring. It is a strong flier, and is often attracted to light. This one has opened its wing cases and is about to take off.

JUMPERS

When confronted with danger, some insects have only one chance to escape and that is by jumping. If the insect is drab-coloured and blends in well with its surroundings, it may not be spotted, but once a predator has it in its sights, the insect may well need to jump for its life. Bright colours on insects often signal that it is poisonous, and some insects have flashy colours that show up on their unfurled hind legs and wings to put off possible attackers. Another defence mechanism is for the hind legs to be covered in spines so that if a hunter traps it, the pain of the encounter forces it to let go.

When an insect jumps, the power comes from the two parts of the hind legs which open up to form a straight line, as the insect pushes off from the ground. Parts of these hind legs are given the same name as those of frogs or humans. The upper part is called the femur, and the lower part is called the tibia. When the insect is at rest, these two long parts of the leg are folded up on themselves. In the grasshopper, the bent hind legs stick up in the air, ready for action.

Young locusts are commonly referred to as

▼ **Flick and click**
When threatened by a hunter, click beetles, such as this one from the Caribbean island of Trinidad, don't run or fly away. Instead they fall to the ground and play dead. Most predators go away, but if they do not, the beetle suddenly flicks itself out of the way (see box below).

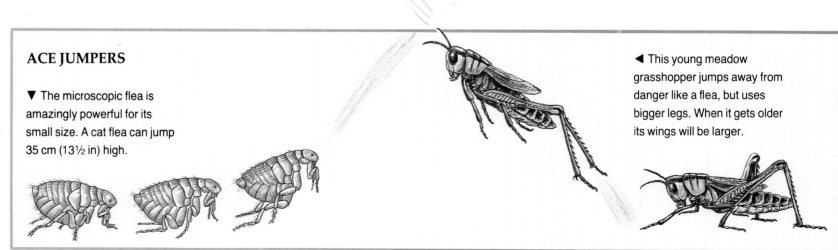

ACE JUMPERS

▼ The microscopic flea is amazingly powerful for its small size. A cat flea can jump 35 cm (13½ in) high.

◄ This young meadow grasshopper jumps away from danger like a flea, but uses bigger legs. When it gets older its wings will be larger.

▼ Visible warning

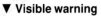

This painted grasshopper from the Mexican desert is very brightly coloured, to warn potential attackers. Its long hind legs are ready for action, but its wings are still too short for flight.

▶ Sudden starts

Leafhoppers and treehoppers are given their names because they hop away from danger. Since surprise is an important part of their escape strategy, they leap in the air unexpectedly, pushing off with both their long hindlegs.

"hoppers". At this stage in their development they do not have wings, and they can only get about by hopping. They normally live together in large colonies numbering several thousands.

Hairs on bodies

Some hopping insects, such as fleas, have special hairs on their head and front of the thorax. They hop on to an animal and "attach" themselves to it with these hairs. It is then very difficult for the host animal to get rid of them.

▼ A click beetle caught in the act of playing dead to avoid an attacker.

▲ The hinged joint between its head and thorax helps a click beetle to somersault. When lying on its back, it arches its body until it can go no further. The body then snaps forward, hurling the beetle into the air.

◀ The way the springtail jumps is explained by its name. Springtails tuck their "tail" underneath their body. When they want to jump the "tail" snaps backward to hurl the insect into the air.

SENSES

Although insects are not intelligent in the same way that people are, they do have very highly developed senses, with excellent powers of vision, an incredible sense of smell, and good touch and feel sensations all over their bodies. The one sense they do lack is good hearing. An insect's brain, although tiny, works rather like a computer, recording and storing the complex and varied information that the insect needs to survive in its habitat, keeping it safe from would-be attackers.

▼ Eyes everywhere
Insects have compound eyes made up of lots of little eyes, each pointing in a slightly different direction. You can see the hundreds of tiny eyes, or facets, which make up the two big compound eyes on this horse fly.

You can see how an insect's brain works by observing the way that it receives information from the sense system it possesses. An insect will rapidly react to danger, either by walking away, jumping, flying, or even falling to the ground and pretending to be dead if the attack is too sudden for flight. You can see an insect's escape mechanism in action if you try to catch a housefly – it *always* flies away. The insect responds to rapid, threatening movement, but slow movement may well prove the solution to catching it.

The sense of smell is one of the most powerful

Inside an insect's compound eye

Facet

Lens

Inside a human eye

Eye muscles

Optic nerve to brain

Optic nerves to brain

LOTS OF LENSES

The little eyes in the compound eye are very much like our own eyes as each has a lens. The insect eye can see shapes and certain colours but with very little detail, probably less detail than we can see with our eyes.

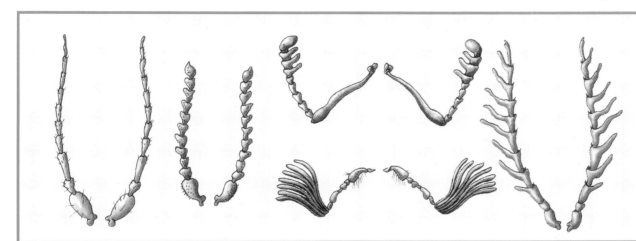

FEELING DIFFERENT

Insects can often be identified by their feelers. They come in all sorts of shapes and sizes, and are called feelers since they have hairs which sense touch, although they are also used for distinguishing different smells.

senses in an insect. Some moths can detect the presence of a mate up to 6 km (4 miles) away. This is because females give off a scent that is carried on the wind, and the male, which normally has larger feelers than the female, picks up this scent like a television aerial picking up broadcasting signals.

Smelling holes

A silkmoth, for example, has 1,700 hairs on its feelers; each hair is like a minute sponge with 2,500 tiny holes in it. Smells carried on the air tumble through the holes and are logged in the insect's brain. If a female is near, the male can then track her down.

▲ Catching the scent
The feelers on this Peruvian beetle are splayed out, allowing scents to be detected over a greater area. The feathery shape of these feelers means that the beetle has a better chance of picking up different smells.

▶ A long feel
The length of the feelers is normally in proportion to the insect's sense of smell. This cricket from Trinidad has exceptionally long feelers, which can be held together as a stick disguise.

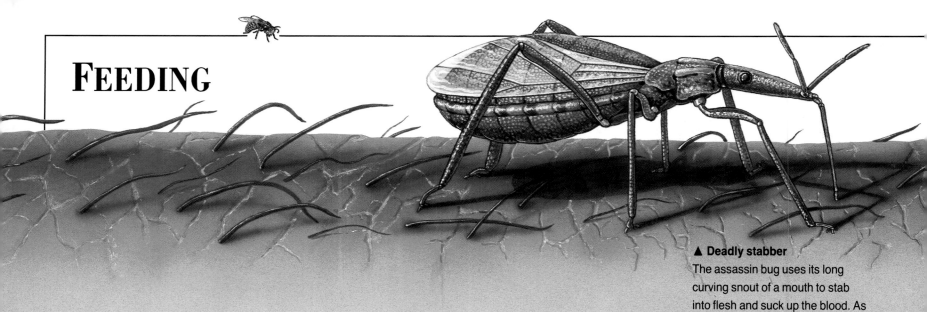

FEEDING

The mouths of bugs and beetles are very different. Bugs have a piercing mouth with which to spear or prick the skin of plants or animals so that they can drink the fluid inside. The piercing mouths of some bugs are extremely fine, rather like sharp needles. Most bugs feed on plant juices but some suck the blood of mammals and other animals. The "sting" which some bugs deliver can feel very uncomfortable. Beetles, on the other hand, have jaws which can cut, bite and crunch.

▲ **Deadly stabber**
The assassin bug uses its long curving snout of a mouth to stab into flesh and suck up the blood. As it stabs, it injects a painkiller so it can feed unnoticed. Bacteria carried by the bug can cause deadly diseases in its victims.

◄ **Flea beetles**
Flea beetles are tiny, very like fleas, and vary from 2 to 5 mm ($\frac{1}{11}$ to $\frac{1}{5}$ in) in length – just slightly larger than a real flea. There are large numbers of them, and they feed on plants, devouring them in a few days. Leaves attacked by flea beetles end up looking rather like skeletons, with only the tough veins left. Flea beetles are sometimes pests, attacking our crops. They come in all sorts of colours, sometimes metallic-looking blues and greens. These red and white flea beetles are eating a leaf in the rainforest of Brazil and leaving their droppings on the remaining food.

▼ Poisonous oil

Oil beetles are so called because they ooze a poisonous oil from their bodies to defend themselves against birds and lizards. Here a South African oil beetle feeds on a morning glory flower.

MOUTHLESS MOTHS

Like bugs, moths and butterflies have long mouthparts that are used to suck up their food as you would suck up drink through a straw (*right*).

Most butterflies and moths have to feed each day to survive. But they only have to survive long enough to mate and lay eggs. This may only take a few days although some species may live for months. A few moths, such as the Indian moon moth, do not even need mouthparts. They reproduce and die so quickly that they don't need to eat.

There are more different types of beetle on earth than any other kind of insect. In fact every fourth insect in the world is a beetle, and they are all voracious feeders with chewing mouth parts. They feed on living and dead plants, and use their tough jaws to chomp through leaves, stems and flowers.

Side to side

Beetles have a completely different way of chewing food from us. Their jaws move from side to side to mash up the food, while ours move up and down. The cutting edges of the beetle's jaws are jagged to make chewing easier. Because they are so numerous and feed so hungrily, many beetles are regarded as pests, especially when they eat the very things we want to grow.

Two particular beetle pests are the Colorado beetle, which feeds on potatoes, and the blossom beetle which feeds on apple and pear flowers.

There are beetles, though, that live a blameless life in the hedgerows and woodlands, and are actually beneficial because they help to break down and recycle last year's leaves as new compost, which plants need for their own growth.

25

HUNTERS

The world of insects is full of creatures that eat plants, but there are also hunter-killers that eat other insects. More often than not, these fierce predators eat their victims alive. They have better senses, are more alert to movement around them and are skilful acrobats, moving in for the kill. Once their prey is caught, they grip it with their spiny legs or crush it in their powerful jaws.

Praying mantis are expert at avoiding being seen. Their weird-looking bodies help them to blend in with the flowers on which they sit while waiting for their lunch to arrive in the form of an insect. So the shape and colour of the mantis combine to make it invisible on the flower. When another insect,

▼ **Drunk dry**
This African robberfly has caught a tough little beetle, but for the beetle there is no escape from certain death, since the robberfly has found a soft chink between its head and its wings to drink its juices.

QUICK GRAB

Quick action is essential if the praying mantis is to catch its food. When an insect gets close, the mantis suddenly lunges and grips it with its spiny front legs, impaling it on the spines.

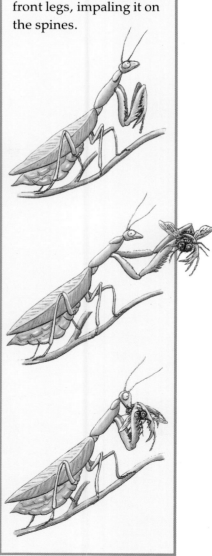

attracted to the flower by its colour, gets too close the mantis lashes out and pins it in one fast movement – faster than your eye can see. The unfortunate victim is then eaten alive, with no attempt to kill it first.

Mating murder

Mating time for the male mantis is a perilous affair. The female will sometimes bite the male's head off in the course of mating. Males tend to be smaller and have learned to be extremely agile to prevent them from losing their heads to the attacking females!

Eaten alive

The familiar ladybird, which looks so gentle, is actually a predator with a hearty appetite for aphids. During its life of three weeks, the ladybird larva eats its way through hundreds of aphids, which curiously do not even try to escape when eaten alive.

TRAPPERS

Ant lions have a unique way of catching small insects. They live in sandy areas and dig out a funnel-shaped hollow, keeping themselves hidden in the sand at the bottom. When an unsuspecting insect trundles along, it falls into the funnel. Since the sides are steep and made of sand, the insect falls to the bottom where the ant lion larva waits with fierce jaws open wide, ready for delivery of its next food parcel.

◄ **In the pink**
This pink praying mantis from Kenya is snacking on a bee fly which came too close. It probably made the fatal mistake of thinking that the mantis was a pink flower.

▲ **Army ants**
Scurrying army ants from Trinidad will pick up and dismember any insects in their path, such as caterpillars, beetles or bugs. The prey are taken back to the nest.

INSECT PROTECTION

I t is survival of the fittest in the big world that small insects live in. Deception is the name of the game that they play. Many insects are green- or brown-coloured so that they blend in with their environment, but others are brightly coloured as a visual warning to predators that they are nasty to eat. The insect's body may also mirror the shape of the plant it is resting on, making a perfect disguise.

▼ **Clever mimic**
Because it mimics the shape and colours of the lycid beetle, which is nasty to eat, the Peruvian moth avoids being attacked. It does not have to hide, as predators will assume it is nasty to eat.

Copying colours and shapes of other animals and plants is called mimicry. The animal that does this is called a mimic, and the animal or plant that is being copied is called the model. It is as if you went to the circus dressed in a clown's outfit and painted your face – everybody would think you were part of the show.

Life-long act

Although you could take the outfit off and clean your face, mimic insects have to keep up the pretence all their lives, as they are always in danger of being caught. If a predator ever detected a mimic, it would gobble it up straightaway.

Mimic insects that are brightly coloured are pretending to be poisonous and dangerous insects, and the colour pattern they copy is often modelled on wasps and bees which is why you see a lot of yellow and black or white and black insects.

The mimic insect trades on the fact that animals will not touch dangerous or poisonous insects. Once a bird has learned the lesson that a particular coloured insect tastes nasty, any similarly coloured insects will get left alone – with luck.

All insects have a tough outer skin, called a cuticle, that protects their soft inner parts, and

which also protects them from the knocks and bumps that they would get while moving around their own habitats. The insect's protective colouring is part of this hard external skeleton, but there are other defences.

Sharp points and smells

Spines, poisonous hairs and vicious backward-facing spurs on its legs all help to protect an insect in the event of an attack, even if the predator manages to pick the insect up in its mouth, as the pain may cause the predator to drop its prey. As a last resort, some insects also let off a bad smell when caught. Stink bugs are so called after the

▼ Thorn bugs

Among the insect bugs there are many kinds that manage to disguise themselves as thorns on stems. These thorn bugs from Peru enjoy safety in numbers, and mimic stems of climbers that are covered in masses of vicious-looking spines. It seems extraordinary to us that an insect can look so like a part of a plant, but this is exactly what is happening here. So disguised, the insects can feed on the plant without fear.

▲ Praying mantis

The praying mantis hides itself by standing almost still, only swaying slightly as if the breeze were stirring a branch.

▲ Green brindled beauty

A freshly-emerged brindled beauty moth has a delicate pattern of mottled green over its splayed-out wings, which helps it to blend in with its background.

▲ Leaf mimic bush cricket

This leaf mimic bush cricket has wings that help it to look like an old leaf complete with veins.

▼ Stick insect

The body of this stick insect, drawn-out like a long piece of plasticine, hides it so well that a hungry bird looking for food will probably miss it.

▲ Leaf insect

The very shape of this insect hides it from predators as long as it stays still – but even a moving leaf may fool a hunter.

▼ Kallima butterfly

Only the undersides of this kallima butterfly from south-east Asia help hide it from predators. When danger passes it can safely open its blue and black wings.

▲ Where are they?

Insects that live in tropical rainforests choose many different things to mimic. They might choose the shape of a straight stick, or of a bent twig. They might take on the colour of tree bark, or of a brown leaf that has fallen from a branch. They might even pretend to be a fresh leaf still hanging on a tree or bush like the butterfly below. There are six other insects hiding in this picture. Can you find them all?

▲ Master of disguise

This stick-insect from Madagascar is hard to see next to the small twig it is mimicking. Stick-insects come in many varied shapes and colours and are particularly clever at blending in with their backgrounds. At least they are safe for as long as they manage to stay still. A moving stick might well draw the attention of a predator.

▼ Like a leaf

This sulphur butterfly fools predators by pretending to be a leaf. It even has the brown spots an old leaf on a tree or bush might have.

defensive smell they employ.

All kinds of animals produce stinging acid as part of their armoury. If you want to experience the effect yourself, you can try picking up a wood ant. You will find that it emits a nasty smelling acid, known as formic acid, from its body, and when you get a whiff of this acid in your nose, it stings for a moment. Imagine how much greater the effect is on a small bird or animal. It is hardly surprising that the wood ant is then left alone by the birds and animals that would otherwise prey on it.

Acid test

Another insect which uses this kind of defensive spray to great effect is the puss moth caterpillar. When frightened, it spits the acid from glands behind its head, which swells up to look larger than it actually is. All the while the caterpillar rears up and waggles over its head the two odd-looking tails that are on the back end of its body to increase the frightening effect.

CHEMICAL ATTACK

Insects have plenty of nasty tricks they can play on their enemies, including all sorts of unpleasant sprays they can squirt in the face of their attackers. The bombardier beetle, for example, taking aim through its legs, squirts a hot, stinging liquid into the face of a shrew.

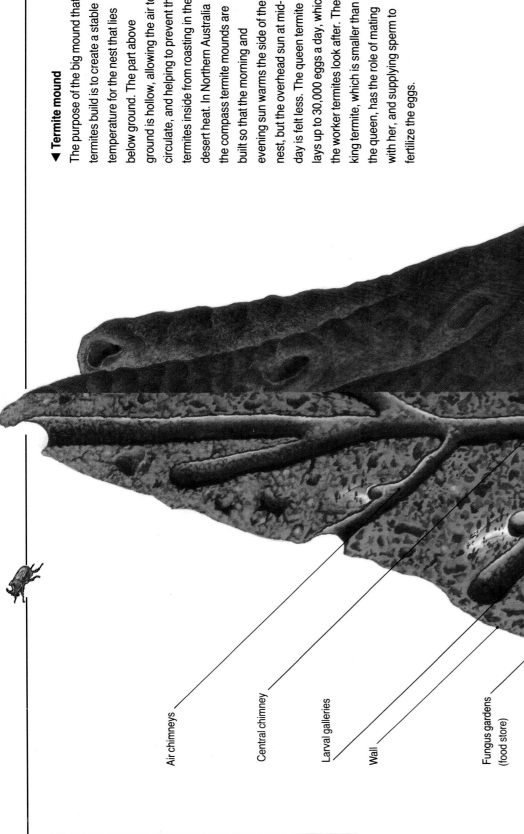

▼ Termite mound

The purpose of the big mound that termites build is to create a stable temperature for the nest that lies below ground. The part above ground is hollow, allowing the air to circulate, and helping to prevent the termites inside from roasting in the desert heat. In Northern Australia the compass termite mounds are built so that the morning and evening sun warms the side of the nest, but the overhead sun at mid-day is felt less. The queen termite lays up to 30,000 eggs a day, which the worker termites look after. The king termite, which is smaller than the queen, has the role of mating with her, and supplying sperm to fertilize the eggs.

Air chimneys

Central chimney

Larval galleries

Wall

Fungus gardens
(food store)

Queen's chamber

Tunnels

▲ Fungus gardens

As many as 10,000 termites can be found in a piece of soil the size of a school desk, all foraging for leaves. They break these into tiny pieces and take them back to the nests, where the leaves are allowed to gather a fungus. The fungus growth provides the ants with food.

▼ Big bouncers

Soldier termites have heads and jaws which are particularly strong. The soldier termites are usually larger than the worker termites, and serve to protect the colony from intruders by chasing them away or killing them.

▼ **Caught in the trap**

Imprisoned in the sharp fangs of this spider, the cricket has no chance of escape. In fact, the spider was probably waiting, head down, ready for an unsuspecting insect to pass very close, and was poised to attack. Spiders inject poison into their prey, which stuns it. The prey is then bound up in the spider's silken thread, and stored in the larder, if it is not eaten straightaway. Although the cricket's green colour blends in with its background when it is still, as soon as it moves it is easy to spot.

▲ **Stock still**

You would not blame any predator who passed this budding plant by. But that would be wrong – these rosea bugs from Madagascar look just like healthy buds on a brown twig – until they move. But when they are still, and particularly when they are grouped together like real buds on a twig, their disguise is perfect.

▲ The combination of red and black colouring spells out danger in the insect kingdom. The day-flying burnet moth would kill any predator that swallowed it, as it contains one of the world's most deadly poisons, cyanide.

▶ Armed to the teeth with poisonous spines and barbs, this caterpillar of a tropical butterfly from Trinidad can feed quite happily on the surface of a leaf in full view of birds and lizards. Even they know how dangerous it is.

▶ The foam on the body of this South African grasshopper, known by its scientific name *Phymateus morbillosus*, provides a double defence. It has a horrible smell and it would poison any predator that tasted it.

INSECT HOMES

Insects that live together can help protect each other. They help each other in everything they do – looking after their young, collecting food, cleaning and tidying up their nest and defending each other against attackers. Honey bees have over 50,000 individuals in a colony, while termites may have 50 times that number.

The structure of the colonies in which social insects live is often highly organized. The nurseries of these insects are no exception. Those of bees and wasps, for example, consist of regimented rows of cells in which the grubs grow up to adulthood. Wasps make their cells out of pieces of wood fibre collected from trees, while honey bees make theirs out of beeswax, a natural product produced from the glands on the undersides of the bees' bodies.

Organized living

A computer could not have designed the neat six-sided cells better. Just how the bees manage to get the angles of the cells precisely right, working in the dark using only their legs and mouth parts, is astonishing. The key to the organization of any bee or wasp colony is teamwork, and all the workers join forces to collect food to feed the grubs.

A delicious drink

Honey bees collect four different things from the outside world: nectar, pollen, water, and resin (from trees). The nectar, which is a sugary substance produced by flowers, is sucked up like water by the worker bees. They keep it in their stomachs until they get back to the hive. Here they regurgitate (spit out) the nectar into combs, where it will turn into honey. Honey mixed with pollen is used to feed the larvae of bees. Water helps the bees make wax from which to build their nests, while the resin is used to seal the combs where the eggs are laid and the honey kept.

Honey bees get very excited when they find a

▶ **Sunbathers**
Wood ants live in large mounds made of leaf litter and plant debris. Some mounds can be up to 1 m (39 in) tall. When the weather warms up in spring, you can see the wood ants swarming over the mound to sunbathe and get warm.

▲ Wasps always make their paper nests in rows facing downwards or sideways. A few workers remain on the nest surface as guards. The grubs can be seen sitting at the bottom of the cells, waiting to be fed by the worker on other insects such as flies.

good supply of nectar. They return to the nest and tell their fellow bees about the new discovery. To do this, they have to communicate three things: the type of flower which has the supply, the compass direction for it, and how far the bees need to go in that direction. Bees only fly a maximum of 3.2 km (2 miles) on the outward flight, 6.4 km (4 miles) overall.

The bees communicate their news as follows: the type of flower is obvious from the pollen sticking to the bees' legs, the direction is given by the angle that the bee takes up on the surface of the honeycomb, and the distance is communicated by a series of body wiggles. You can compare it to people giving directions to an unfamiliar place, moving their hand to point in different directions. Bees live a complicated, social life compared to other insects that live alone. However some solitary

▲ Who's got hairy legs?
The hairy-legged mining bee, so called after the golden hairs which cover its legs, is widespread in Europe. It looks dangerous but, in fact, it is harmless. Unlike honey bees, it makes its home in burrows in the ground where it breeds.

WILD BEES' NEST

Before people started to keep bees in hives, honey bees lived quite happily in their own nests, which they made in hollow trees and rock crevices. In a hive, the bees are better protected from disease and bad weather. When bees leave the hive in search of food, they fly a direct line to the source of food. Their memory is so good that if the hive is moved just a few finger-breadths, the bees will keep returning to the original spot.

MERCY MISSION

Dung beetles are common in many countries and serve a very useful purpose. They break up all sorts of animal dung that would otherwise litter the ground. They use it as a source of food for their young, chopping up and rolling the dung into balls. They put these balls in with their eggs. They lay the eggs in a small lair they build beneath piles of dung. Tunnels connect the different "rooms" the eggs are laid in.

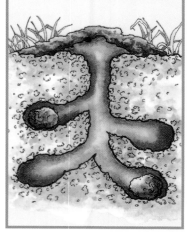

The cherry gall on an oak leaf is the home of the gall-wasp, as it progresses from egg through larva and pupa to adult. The gall itself is caused by the cells that the plant produces in reaction to the insect's eggs laid in its tissues.

Plant tissues

Insect larva

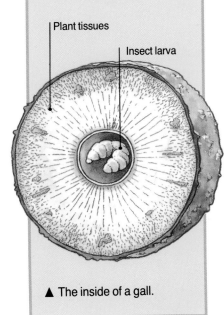

▲ The inside of a gall.

insects still make homes. In some cases these insects make use of what nature provides (see the box on galls). Other insects, including many beetles, live for a time deep within the branches and trunks of trees and bushes, until they emerge for the last phase of their lives.

What a gall!

Galls form on many kinds of shrub and tree, and are caused either by tiny insects, fungi, microscopic mites, bacteria, or viruses. One familiar gall in the forests of Europe and North America is the Rose pin cushion, which is caused by a tiny gall wasp. Other galls are produced by small moths and flies that make their homes between the upper and lower surfaces of leaves, a home known as the "leaf mine".

▲ Clumsy bumblebees
Bumblebees should not be able to fly, according to some scientists. The reason they give is that the bumblebee's body is rather chunky and heavy in relation to the size of the two pairs of wings. The bumblebees manage because their thorax (middle part) is full of muscles which power the small wings. Although they normally fly slowly, they are able to change speed when disturbed and move much faster. Over thousands of years the foxglove has produced flowers that are ideally suited to bumblebees, and they alone go up to the finger-shaped flowers to take the nectar, while pollinating the plant as they do so.

FRESHWATER INSECTS

Water presents no problems for insects as a place to live in, and many grow up in the water before turning into adults that fly in the air. Dragonflies, mayflies, alderflies, and caddis flies all breed in water and then fly away as adults.

How easy is it for insects to live in water? It depends on where you are in the insect order. Big, fierce, and aggressive insects do very well. Among these are the larvae of dragonflies, called nymphs. During the nymph's life underwater it catches and eats all sorts of other aquatic insects (those that live in the water). Its fearsome mouth also enables the nymph to make a meal out of a tadpole.

Jet swimmers

The dragonfly nymphs can zoom through the water astonishingly fast, using a form of jet propulsion – they take in water and squeeze it out of their abdomen.

▲ Fearless hunter
A dragonfly nymph makes a meal out of a damselfly. These nymphs are not afraid to tackle any likely-looking prey, even if it is much bigger.

▲ Snorkelling larvae
Mosquito larvae breathe directly from the air using a straw-like tube that pierces the surface of the water. The larvae spend most of their time near the surface, but will wiggle rapidly to lower depths when danger threatens.

◄ ► Great divers
If it chose, the great diving beetle could give humans a nasty nip. It has vicious jaws, normally reserved for attacking tadpoles, small fish, and other insects. It breathes oxygen that gets trapped in its body hairs. Great diving beetles live for about two years.

▼ Circling beetles

Whirligigs are scavengers. They can usually be found swimming round and round in circles on the surfaces of ponds, waiting for other insects to fall in the water. They are always found in groups.

▼ Rowing the backstroke

The backswimmer or water boatman rows its way through the water using its long back legs. However, it has trouble staying under. It keeps floating back to the surface after each stroke, and has to push itself back underneath with its legs.

THEY'VE GOT LEGS

Pond skaters (above) "skate" on the water with the greatest of ease using their long legs. Pond skaters have piercing jaws. A whole gang will gather around a potential meal, such as a moth or caterpillar, that falls in the water. They fiercely probe the prey to suck out the juices.

The extra long hindlegs of the water boatman (*below*) earn it its name. It uses them like oars, but more efficiently.

▶ Homebuilder
The caddis fly larva spends much of its time on the bed of the stream collecting bits and pieces that flow by to build its home from.

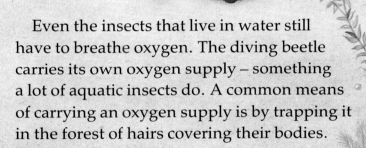

Even the insects that live in water still have to breathe oxygen. The diving beetle carries its own oxygen supply – something a lot of aquatic insects do. A common means of carrying an oxygen supply is by trapping it in the forest of hairs covering their bodies.

Fishy insects

Insects that do not visit the surface for oxygen have gills like fish – frilly membranes over which the water flows, and which allow the oxygen in the water to be absorbed into the animal's body. Insects with gills include the larvae of caddis flies, mayflies, alder-flies, dragonflies, and damselflies.

The oxygen that these insects depend on is given off by healthy green plants and dissolves in the water. Fewer green plants means fewer insects.

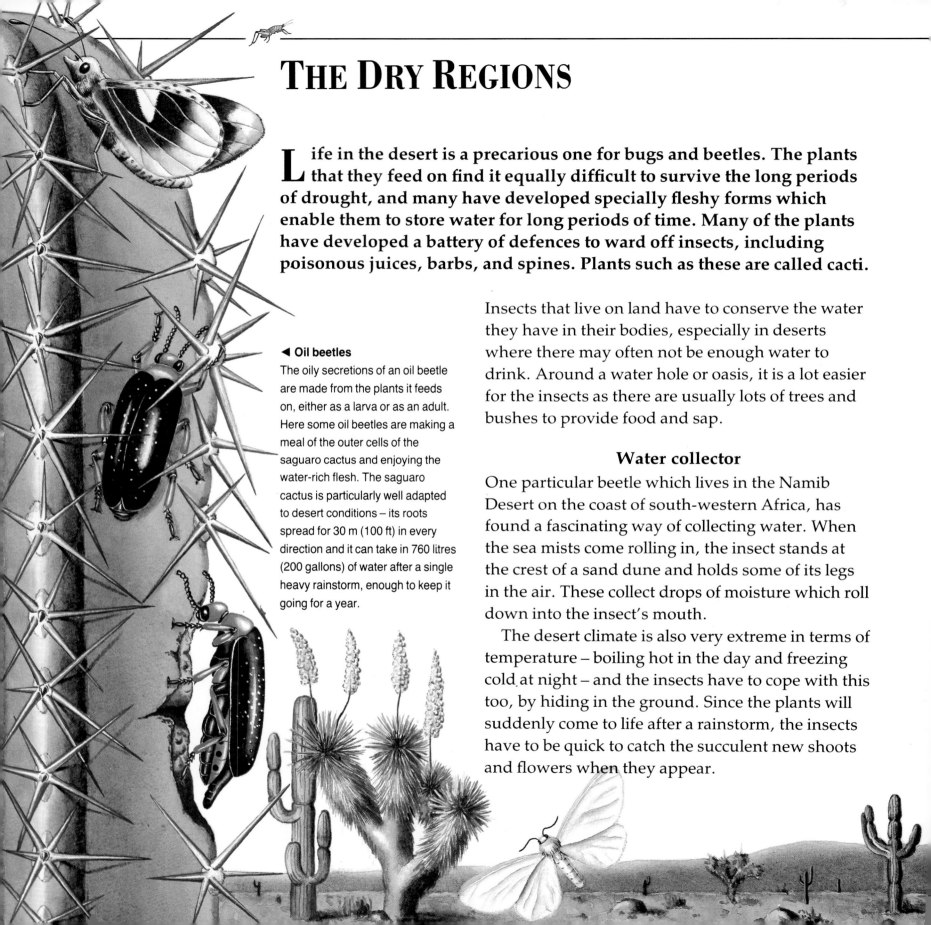

THE DRY REGIONS

Life in the desert is a precarious one for bugs and beetles. The plants that they feed on find it equally difficult to survive the long periods of drought, and many have developed specially fleshy forms which enable them to store water for long periods of time. Many of the plants have developed a battery of defences to ward off insects, including poisonous juices, barbs, and spines. Plants such as these are called cacti.

Insects that live on land have to conserve the water they have in their bodies, especially in deserts where there may often not be enough water to drink. Around a water hole or oasis, it is a lot easier for the insects as there are usually lots of trees and bushes to provide food and sap.

Water collector

One particular beetle which lives in the Namib Desert on the coast of south-western Africa, has found a fascinating way of collecting water. When the sea mists come rolling in, the insect stands at the crest of a sand dune and holds some of its legs in the air. These collect drops of moisture which roll down into the insect's mouth.

The desert climate is also very extreme in terms of temperature – boiling hot in the day and freezing cold at night – and the insects have to cope with this too, by hiding in the ground. Since the plants will suddenly come to life after a rainstorm, the insects have to be quick to catch the succulent new shoots and flowers when they appear.

◀ **Oil beetles**
The oily secretions of an oil beetle are made from the plants it feeds on, either as a larva or as an adult. Here some oil beetles are making a meal of the outer cells of the saguaro cactus and enjoying the water-rich flesh. The saguaro cactus is particularly well adapted to desert conditions – its roots spread for 30 m (100 ft) in every direction and it can take in 760 litres (200 gallons) of water after a single heavy rainstorm, enough to keep it going for a year.

DESERT EGGS

An insect egg contains all the material needed to make an adult insect. So the egg is a very important capsule which must survive through to hatching. No wonder female insects invest so much time and energy in finding a safe and secure place for all their eggs. In the desert the main job of the tough egg shell is to stop the egg losing much water. Water loss can mean death in the desert. Female insects lay their eggs out of the way of the full sun, usually in cracks in the cacti, in flowers, under leaves, or underground.

The eggs may remain in their hiding place for a long time. When it rains – which it does only rarely in deserts – plants make their flowers and fruits quickly to take advantage of the water before the sun has dried it up.

The insect eggs hatch, and attack the now-juicy plants. The adult insects reproduce quickly, before the desert dryness returns. The eggs they lay then stay hidden until it rains again.

▲ A "night owl"
In deserts many beetles, such as this jewel beetle from South Africa, are active at night to avoid the extreme heat of the day. Others bury themselves deep in the flesh of plants or flowers and feed on vital moist plant material.

▼ Superbly camouflaged
Escaping detection in a desert is important as food is always scarce. A brightly-coloured beetle would attract attention. This one, known by its scientific name *Sepiodium tricuspidatum*, is hard to spot against the sand.

▲ Flexible living
This cicada makes its home in the dry regions of central Mexico. It lives on the small, scrubby trees that grow there.

THE TEEMING RAINFORESTS

I f you visited the rainforests of the world you would find more insects there than in any other kind of forest. The reason is simple – there are so many more types of trees, shrubs, flowers and other animals to provide food for them. Yet despite hundreds of years of researching life on earth, we know little about insect life here. Even though scientists have created long lists of tropical insect species, there are probably still millions to be discovered.

▼ Young bugs
A group of cottonstrainer bugs gather together for protection in the Brazilian rainforest. The black buds on their backs are their wings, which are just starting to grow.

One of the reasons scientists know less than they would like about tropical insects is because most of the insects live in the tops of trees. Up there, at least 50 m (160 ft) above the floor of the jungle, is not the easiest place for people to find them! Although visitors to the rainforest rarely climb all the way up the trees, the scientists who study insect life occasionally build a ropewalk through the treetops. Then they are able to see and photograph some of the bugs that never come down to the ground.

▲ Hiding in Madagascar
The brownish hairs on this weevil are camouflage to protect it from predators. It lives in Madagascar, off south-east Africa.

▶ Big nose
Weevils are types of beetle. They have long noses called rostrums. This one is longer than most. It belongs to a leaf-rolling weevil, also from Madagascar's rainforests.

◀ Fast developers
Plant bugs, such as these lantern fly bugs, grow fast in rainforests as they suck up plant juices through their straw-like mouth parts.

The easiest place to study insects in rainforests is the riverbank. If you walked along, you would see the insects drinking water from the damp sandbanks. Thirsty male butterflies can often be found there.

Sweet and homely attractions

Beetles, ants, and moths are attracted to the sweet juices which flow from damaged tree trunks, and scientists can often study them there at close quarters. The old wood of tree trunks is recycled by termites and wood-boring beetles into their nests.

◀ Drinking on the alert
With its tongue outstretched this bright skipper from the Peruvian rainforest is drinking water from damp sand. Even so, it is alert and ready to fly in a second if a predator should happen by.

▶ Two beauties
This butterfly, known by its scientific name of *Amarynthis menaria menaria,* flies up to a passion flower.

◀ Which way is up?
By distracting attention away from the main juicy and delicate parts of their bodies, these flag-legged bugs from the Costa Rican rainforests confuse predators. Sure that they are safe, they carry on drinking the fluids from passion fruit buds.

FROM CRADLE TO GRAVE

Insects grow up in one of two ways. Some change their entire appearance one or more times in the course of their lives. This is known as complete metamorphosis. Others simply grow until their outer hard casing or skeleton can grow no more, then burst out of it and grow a replacement skeleton very quickly. This is known as incomplete metamorphosis. The lifestyle and place where the insect lives helps to determine which of the two it will follow.

BUG LIFE CYCLES

All bugs, such as the assassin bugs shown here hatch looking like miniature adults. This is the nymph stage (right). As the nymph grows (below) it sheds its old skin and begins to fill out its new skin. The bug continues the cycle by feeding and growing.

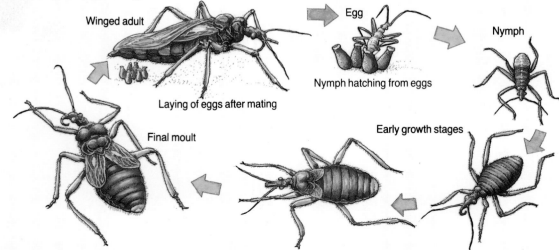

Winged adult

Laying of eggs after mating

Egg

Nymph hatching from eggs

Nymph

Final moult

Early growth stages

Aphid bugs (the group that includes greenflies and blackflies) can reproduce more quickly than most other kinds of insect. And they do not always need males to do so. In the spring, the female aphids (who do not lay eggs) give birth to fully-formed young and amazingly some of these young have their own young inside them as they are born. In warm weather aphids reproduce even more quickly.

This extraordinarily rapid succession of life cycles is nature's way of ensuring that insects do not miss the best time for feeding. For aphids, this is when tender young shoots of plants start to emerge.

Almost all insects start their lives as an egg. The egg might be buried underground, or it might be stuck to a leaf, or it might be hidden somewhere else. What happens next will depend on the kind of insect the egg contains.

Changing shape

The insects whose life cycle is called incomplete metamorphosis emerge from the egg as a nymph (see the box on the shield bug, opposite), which looks a lot like an adult, but there are differences. Slowly, after each successive stage of skin-shedding and growth the nymph looks more and more like an adult. It sprouts wings and becomes bigger until finally it is fully grown and can fly and reproduce.

Those insects that undergo a complete metamorphosis do not have an initial nymph stage. They hatch from the egg as a larva, often looking like a white worm. From this, you would not expect them to grow and change as they do. A larva eats and grows, shedding its skin in the same way as a nymph, but without changing its form.

The next step

Once the larva has grown through several stages, it turns into a pupa. A pupa doesn't eat, and can

GROWING UNDERGROUND

There are over 3000 different kinds of cicada in the world. Unlike most other insects, cicadas take several years to grow from a nymph to an adult.

During this time the nymphs live and feed underground. Just before its final moult, the nymph crawls out of the soil and up a tree or plant stem. Here the adult begins to climb out of the skin (*top right*). Its wings begin unfolding (*bottom right*). They are still damp and useless. The cicada waits for its wings to dry before it can fly (*far right*). At this point it is easy for predators to catch.

hardly move. It is usually hidden in a case. There it will be comparatively safe from predators, who may not realize what it is. An insect can be a pupa for a few days or for several months. But finally the pupa will split open and a fully-grown adult will emerge. This body is initially very soft, but the outside skin soon hardens.

The grown-up insect

Adult insects can live as short a time as a couple of hours, others survive for several years. Whatever the length of life, they all do much the same thing. They spend some of their time searching for food but their main aim is to produce more young. The insects that live together in large groups have to build and maintain their nests, and sometimes have to look after the young of their queen.

Egg making

The most important job for an insect to do during its life is to reproduce itself. For most insects to reproduce, it is necessary for the male to find a female and mate with her. Afterwards, the female hunts out a suitable spot, and puts the eggs there. A female butterfly, for example, lays her eggs on the type of leaf which the caterpillars will feed on.

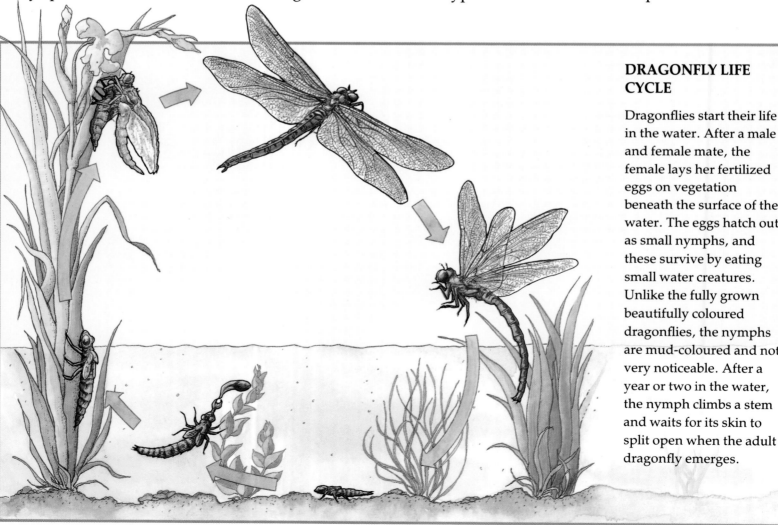

DRAGONFLY LIFE CYCLE

Dragonflies start their life in the water. After a male and female mate, the female lays her fertilized eggs on vegetation beneath the surface of the water. The eggs hatch out as small nymphs, and these survive by eating small water creatures. Unlike the fully grown beautifully coloured dragonflies, the nymphs are mud-coloured and not very noticeable. After a year or two in the water, the nymph climbs a stem and waits for its skin to split open when the adult dragonfly emerges.

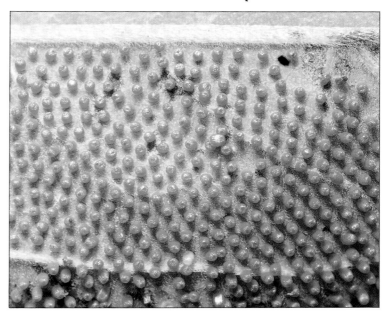

▲ Hidden eggs
Butterfly eggs have no defence against predators, so some are disguised. These are of the acraeid butterfly from Trinidad.

► Broken image
This sweet potato hawkmoth caterpillar feeds securely. The dark bands on its body help by breaking up the image predators see.

▲ Big from little
The caterpillar that emerges from a butterfly's egg is not very big. But it keeps eating until it turns into a fully-grown caterpillar hundreds of times bigger and fatter than when it hatched. Its colours begin to fade just before it turns into a chrysalis.

▼ Making a home
All caterpillars can produce silk thread, and when the caterpillar begins to turn into a chrysalis, it first spins itself a place on which to rest. Then, it makes a silken girdle to strap it to this base. Once that is done it sheds its caterpillar skin and reveals a tough chrysalis coat underneath.

HELPFUL INSECTS

A surprising number of insects work hard to be our friends. Honey bees serve us by pollinating the flowers we grow in our gardens, and they also make delicious honey. Flies and butterflies also help to pass flower pollen around on their visits to flowers in search of food, helping to pollinate them. Insects that eat other insects which, in turn, are pests also help people: for example, ladybirds eat the aphids that destroy many of the plants raised by gardeners.

▼ **Gardener's friend**
The hornet is simply a large wasp, and although it looks mean, it actually helps people in many ways; early in the year its diet includes many of the pests disliked by gardeners, including caterpillars, sawflies, and aphids.

There are many products on the market which will kill or chase away insects. However, not all insects are harmful to us, and we certainly don't want to drive them all away.

Bees, and other friends

We count the honey bee among our insect friends, even if it is equipped with a nasty sting. The bees produce honey, which we share with them, and other insects also make things we can use, such as the silkworm and its silk.

However, would you count the wasp as a friend?

SWEET BEES

Honey bees take the sweet nectar they find in flowers and turn it into honey. Some people keep specially built beehives with combs (right) for the honey. Once or twice a year they remove some of the honeycomb as their share of the bees' work.

FUSSY EATERS

The silkworm moth caterpillar eats only mulberry leaves. These leaves are poisonous to nearly all other insects. All caterpillars make silk, but those of the silkworm produce up to 620 m (2000 ft) of silk in each of their cocoons (right). People have learned to unravel the silk and weave it into cloth, which is among the finest there is.

▼ Unladylike ladybirds
Ladybirds are a kind of beetle. They and their larvae are actually hardened killers who eat their way through hundreds of aphids.

Probably not, but you would be wrong. Wasps may scavenge for food around your lunch, but some species also hunt down that other unwanted mealtime guest, the fly.

Cleaner killers

Using predatory insects, such as ladybirds and wasps, to kill pesky ones is much less harmful to the environment than spraying chemicals. Chemicals harm other creatures, build up in the environment and take a long time to lose their effects.

LITTLE HELPERS

The tiny wasps are very helpful to us. They lay their eggs inside caterpillars which feed on our garden vegetables. When the eggs hatch the wasps' larvae feed off the caterpillar's flesh (right), eventually killing it.

Creatures which live on or in another animal, and get their food from it, are called parasites.

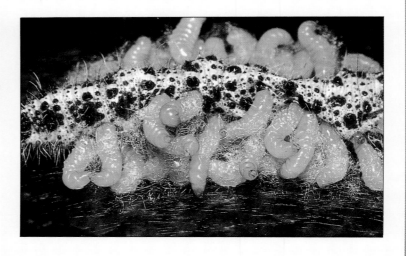

INSECTS IN DANGER

Unfortunately, people have been greedy or foolish enough to destroy many of the habitats that a whole host of insects thrive in. Extinction is caused by natural means as well. If a bird predator comes along and eats the last remaining larvae of an endangered beetle species, then the beetle will become extinct. Endangered species are those which are one step away from extinction. In other words, unless they receive our help, they could disappear for ever.

The rate at which natural habitats throughout the world are disappearing is alarming. The area of a school playing field is being destroyed, each minute, day and night. It is destroyed as country-side is cleared to make way for new houses, schools, factories, and roads. The natural surroundings of countless insects and other wildlife are consumed, in order to satisfy our own needs. So the plants and animals either die or take off for new habitats, if they can. Is this really fair?

Stopping the damage

Tropical rainforests and jungles have more bugs and beetles than any other type of habitat on earth, but they are being destroyed by people who want to plant crops to feed their families, or who want to use the trees to make furniture. Although some damage to rainforests is done by the people who are trying to live there, much more is caused by people who want to make money out of the habitat.

One way that you can help to try to save the rainforests is by making sure that you or your parents do not buy things that properly belong in the forests, such as imported animals or the wood from the trees.

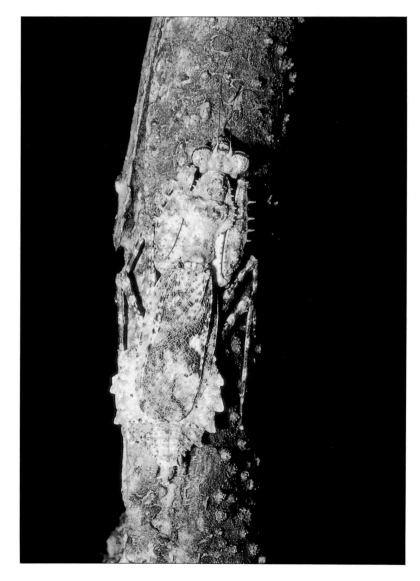

▼ **Rare and strange**
There are only a few records of this praying mantis which lives in the rainforests of Madagascar. If the rainforests are cut down, this insect, and thousands of others that survive in these habitats, will die.

◄ Where is it now?

This monkey-hopper from the rainforests of Peru is only known from this photograph. The forests where it lives have been destroyed, and the insect may now be endangered or even extinct. With a bit of luck, it may still survive in another rainforest somewhere else. However, we will only know for sure if someone else finds it. Scientists interested in insects (entomologists, or bug-hunters) visit many parts of the world to try to find new species, and to discover whether existing ones are still surviving.

PROTECTED BY LAW

Thousands of insects around the world are endangered, and many may suddenly become extinct tomorrow. In Britain, over 500 insects are listed as being endangered, but only a small number are protected by the Wildlife and Countryside Act. The heath fritillary (below, a mating pair) is one of the lucky ones. Its habitat is also protected. The United States have passed laws protecting five sorts of beetles including the American burying beetle and the tooth cave mold beetle.

▲ Threatened beauty

This butterfly is one of several kinds of apollo butterflies that are very rare, partly because they are so beautiful. People kill them to put on display in cabinets or picture frames. They are equally threatened by the destruction of their habitat. They breed on the tops of high mountains, many of which are being turned into resorts for skiing. While people are having a good time on holiday, do they think about how the plants, on which the caterpillars of the apollo butterflies had fed, were destroyed to make room?

25 Essential Facts About Bugs, Beetles, and Other Insects

E ven the world's greatest bug-hunters do not know all the fascinating details about every bug and beetle in the world. This fact-packed bug and beetle kit gives you a handy summary of the most interesting information about these fascinating creatures.

1 Millions and millions

There are over 1 million different kinds, or species, of insects so far given names on earth. Entomologists (meaning "insect-students") believe at least another 1 million wait to be discovered and named.

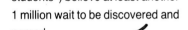

2 One in four

There are more different kinds of beetle in the world than any other insect. In fact, every fourth insect on earth is a beetle.

3 25 a day!

There are over 4,000 species of aphid in the world, and "mother" aphids can give birth to 25 young each day. We would be quickly swamped by aphids if most were not eaten by predators.

4 True bugs

Although the name "bugs" is often used for any creepy-crawly or any insect, it is correctly used for insects called "true bugs" that have piercing mouthparts.

5 Blood suckers

There are several bugs that are blood-sucking, such as the bed bug. Blood-sucking bugs can pass on deadly diseases to people when they use their mouthparts to pierce a person's skin.

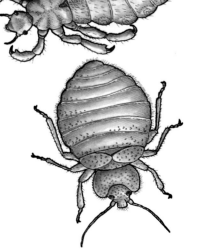

6 The oldest of the lot

The oldest living insects are the nymphs of some cicadas, a kind of bug. They live underground eating roots for up to 22 years before they come up as adults.

7 The weightiest beetle

The heaviest beetle in the world is the goliath beetle from equatorial Africa. It not only looks awesome, but weighs up to 100 g (3½ oz) and is up to 12 cm (5 in) long.

8 Weird and wonderful

The most weird-shaped bugs are those that look like plant thorns complete with prickles on the end of their "spines".

9 Heaviest swimmers

The heaviest aquatic insect in the world is the giant water-bug from South America which is 12 cm (5 in) long and weighs 5.5 g (2 oz).

10 Longest of the lot

The longest beetles in the world are the Hercules beetles from Central America. They reach up to 18 cm (7½ in) long.

11 Air express
Aphids can drift in the wind and be carried several thousand feet into the sky, only to be dropped by the wind in another country having crossed hundreds of miles.

12 Noisy fliers
The whining a mosquito makes is caused by it breaking the sound barrier with its wings, beating at 1,000 times a second.

13 Bug anti-freeze
Several insects that live at the tops of mountains or in the cold Arctic have a natural anti-freeze in their blood which keeps them from freezing to death.

14 Scented on the wind
Insects use their sense of smell more than people, and in some moths the males can detect a female 6 km (3½ miles) away.

15 Hairy smellers
The antennae of insects have a very powerful sense of smell. The silkmoth has 1,700 hairs on its antennae, and on each hair are 2,500 holes for the smell to be detected in.

16 Flea rockets
When the flea jumps it accelerates as fast as a space rocket re-entering the earth's atmosphere.

17 Call on the law
The American burying beetle is considered an endangered species. But the US Congress has passed a law protecting them and their habitat.

18 TV eyes
The dragonfly has exceptional powers of vision and each of its two compound eyes has 30,000 smaller eye units. We imagine it looks at the equivalent of 60,000 tiny television sets, each pointing in a slightly different direction.

19 Loudest singers
The loudest of all insects is the male cicada which sings so loudly for a mate that people can hear its resonant song up to 0.5 km (¼ mile) away.

20 Bad bugs and beetles
Many bugs and beetles are pests. They eat our crops. The boll weevil, which eats the seed pods of cotton plants, and the Colorado potato beetle, which eats potato plants, are two examples.

21 Talk to me
Honey bees actually have a kind of language. In the hive they can tell other bees the compass direction (north, south, east, west) and distance to certain flowers.

22 Clever defenders
Some insects can defend themselves when attacked. One common way is to spray the predator in the face with formic acid. This is done by the puss moth caterpillar and the bombardier beetle.

23 Phew!
Many bugs keep predators away by their smells. Stink bugs make a kind of oil that clings to the plants they visit. Not many predators will want to follow such an unpleasant odour around.

24 Strong jaw tactics
Beetles often have huge jaws, the stag beetles for example. One longhorn beetle can lift in its jaws a piece of old wood nearly 200 times heavier than itself, but the record goes to a scarab beetle which can lift something 850 times heavier than itself.

25 Losing their heads
Male praying mantis have to watch out – the female likes to bite his head off during mating. To nip out of the way of her jaws very quickly, he is therefore small, elusive, and very nervous.

GLOSSARY

(Note: Words in *italics* refer to other entries in the Glossary.)

Abdomen The third and last part of an insect's body, where most of the digestive system and the reproductive *organs* are. It also has breathing holes in its side.

Antennae A pair of *organs* on the insect's head that are sometimes very long. They are also called feelers. They can both "feel" and smell very well.

Aphid A common true bug that has *mouthparts* used for piercing and drinking the juices of tender stems and leaves.

Arthropod Animals such as insects, *spiders*, woodlice, and crabs. All of them have legs with several moving joints and a hard skeleton on the outside of their body.

Aquatic Insects that do their *breeding* in water.

Beetle An insect with biting or chewing *mouthparts* and hard wing cases, or elytra.

Breeding The process of courting and mating with a partner, and laying eggs or giving birth to young.

Bug A word many people use to describe any insect, but it also refers to a special group of insects called "true" bugs that have piercing *mouthparts*.

Camouflage The way some insects are coloured or shaped to blend in with the plants, trees, or soils they live among.

Caterpillar The second stage, before the *pupa* stage, in the life history of a butterfly or moth.

Cells (1) The basic living unit from which all plants and animals are built. An egg is a single cell – even a chicken egg. (2) The compartments of a bee hive or wasp's nest, usually six-sided, where the eggs develop.

Chrysalis see *Pupa*.

Colony A group of *social insects* living together in a nest. A termite mound contains a colony.

Compound eyes A pair of eyes on the head, each of which is made up of thousands of smaller eye-units.

Conservation The way people protect plants and animals in their *habitats*. Keeping the *habitat* as little changed as possible is most important in the conservation of any plant or animal.

Cuticle The hard outer part of an insect. It is covered with a fine layer of wax as a protection from the *environment*.

Ecology The study of plants and animals living in their *habitats*. Ecologists are people who study ecology.

Eggs The first stage in the life cycle of most types of insects. The shapes and colours of eggs can often tell you what *species* it belongs to.

Endangered A word used to describe a living thing, such as an insect, that may soon suffer *extinction*.

Environment An area of several different types of *habitats*. Whether an environment is a desert, a jungle, a grassland, or something else will depend on the area's weather and soil.

Extinction The name for what happens to a *species* that has completely died out, or become extinct. Many insects have suffered extinction, and there are many *species* that are *endangered*.

Fertilization The process during which the female *egg* is penetrated by a male *sperm* and a new individual starts to grow.

Glow-worm The glow-worm is the *larva* of a *beetle*. It is therefore an insect, not a worm. Only the female glows – to attract a male for courtship and mating.

Habitat The name used for a place where animals live surrounded by specific kinds of plants. The choice of these plants is decided by the soil and climate of the place. It can be large or small.

Hibernation The way some animal *species* survive cold winters. Many insects hibernate underground or in fallen logs from the autumn to the spring. They slow down their heart beats and do not eat. They may hibernate in either the *egg*, *larva*, *pupa*, or adult stage, according to the *species*.

Hoppers The name given to the *nymphs* of grasshoppers and crickets. Their wings are not fully grown, and they hop along when searching for food or to escape danger.

Hyperparasite see *Parasite*.

Invertebrate A name for all animals that do not have a backbone, including worms, snails, and crabs. Insects are invertebrates.

Jaws Hard *mouthparts* that some insects have for chomping through plant material or the tough outside skeleton of other insects.

Larva The second stage in an insect's development after the egg. All those insects which have a *pupa*, also have a larva commonly called the *caterpillar*.

Mammal A warm-blooded animal which has hair or fur, including whales, deer, mice, and rats. The young are suckled at the breast.

Mating When a female and a male animal of the same *species* come together, and the male's sperm fertilizes the female's eggs, so these can develop into babies.

Metamorphosis The change in form that insects experience as they grow up. There are two types, one where development includes a *pupa* (complete metamorphosis), and one where it does not (incomplete metamorphosis).

Mimicry The way some kinds of insects pretend to be another kind by having similar colours, similar shapes, and similar behaviour.

Mouthparts The parts of the insect body that cut, pierce, or dab at food.

Nymph The early stage of those insects that do not have a *pupa* stage. *Eggs* hatch into nymphs which have the same shape as the adult, but much much smaller.

Organ A part of the body that performs a specific task or tasks. The heart is an organ that pumps blood.

Organism A living thing, such as a plant or an animal, made up of *cells*.

Parasite An insect (or other living thing) which lives on or in another *organism*, called the host. The

parasite feeds on the host, and may harm or even kill it. If a parasite does kill the host, it is usually because the parasite has no further use for it or has outgrown it. A *hyper-parasite* behaves the same way a parasite does except that its host is always already a parasite.

Pollination The taking of pollen from the male part of one flower to the female part of a flower, usually on a different plant. This is often done by an insect such as a bee.

Predator An animal that catches and eats another animal. Predators are usually armed with powerful claws and jaws, and can see well.

Prey An animal that is hunted by a *predator*.

Pseudoscorpions A group of tiny *invertebrates* that look like scorpions with large pincers. They are not insects, but closely related to spiders.

Pupa The stage of an insect's life during which the *larva* stops feeding and encloses itself in a case while it forms its body into its adult shape. Often the pupa *hibernates* and the adult hatches in the spring.

Rainforest Forests in *tropical* places around the Equator in Asia, Africa, and South America.

Scavenger An animal that explores its habitat to find live or dead food

to eat. Ants, the devil's coach horse beetle, and scorpion flies are examples of insect scavengers.

Secretion A variety of fluids that are produced by *cells*. Secretions might be used to attract insects for *pollination* or *mating*, or to keep predators away.

Siphon A small tube that some insects living in water have so that they can breathe air. The siphon sticks up out the water, while the rest of the body remains under the water. *Aquatic larvae* and *pupae* all have siphons for taking in oxygen from the air.

Social insect A kind of insect that lives in a very large group. Social insects are usually divided into different classes by their role in the *colony*. Ants and honey bees are social insects.

Solitary insect A type of insect that normally lives on its own, or in a male-female pair.

Species A single kind or type of animal or plant. Members of a species look and behave much the same as each other, and they can breed with one another. But a member of one species cannot breed with a member of another.

Sperm A sex *cell* produced by male animals, used to fertilise the egg of a female. Males usually produce millions of sperms.

Spiders A group of *invertebrates* having four pairs of legs. Spiders are not insects, although they are found living in the same *habitats*.

Spiracles The openings along the side of an insect. Insects breathe through them. They are easily seen in caterpillars.

Thorax The middle part of an insect's body. The legs and wings stick out from this part. It contains powerful muscles for movement and flight.

Toxic Anything that is poisonous. Some insects, such as oil beetles, use plant poisons, making themselves toxic. They absorb the poisons, which do them no harm, when they eat.

Tropics The warmest regions of the Earth, found to either side of the Equator. Insects love the hot and humid weather found there.

Vector An *organism* such as an insect that transmits a disease, from an infected person to an uninfected one. The disease organism slips into people via the insect's saliva when it sucks their blood. Mosquitos and assassin bugs are frequently vectors of disease.

Weevil A group of beetles that can all be identified by a long snout. Many weevils are pests, destroying people's crops.

INDEX

(Page numbers in *italics* refer to illustrations and captions.)

A

abdomen *14*, 14
acid, for defence 30
acraeid butterfly, eggs *45*
alder flies *11*, 36
Amarynthis menaria menaria 41
antlions 27
ants 13, *15*
aphids, reproduction 42
apollo butterflies *51*
army ants *27*
assassin bugs *24*
automatic responses *14*

B

backswimmer *see* water boatman
bacteria, carrying disease 49
bed bugs 13, *49*, 49
bees 19, 33
    see also honey bees
beetle pests *24*, 25
beetles 10, 12, *13*, 13
    short flights only *19*
biting louse *11*
black ant *10*
blood suckers 49
bloody-nosed beetle *13*
blossom beetle 25
body lice *49*, 49
bombardier beetle *30*, 30
bow-winged grasshopper *13*
breathing tubes *36*
brown lacebug *11*
bugs 10, *13*
    piercing mouthparts 15
bumblebees *35*
bush crickets *14*, *29*, *45*
butterflies *12*, 12, 17, 19, *25*, *29*,
    45, 45
    endangered 51, 51
    feeding 25
    wings of 18

C

cabbage white butterfly 17
cacti *38*, 38
caddis flies *10*, 36
camouflage 10, *39*, *40*, *45*
cardinal beetle 16
cat fleas *20*
caterpillars 13, *45*
    see also silk worms
chemical attack *30*, 30
chemical sprays 48
chrysalis *45*
cicadas *11*, 19, *39*
    final moult *43*, 43
claws 15
click beetles *20*, 21
cockchafer beetle *19*
    wings 16–17
cockroaches 13
colonies, of social insects 32–3
Colorado beetle 25
common blue butterfly *12*
compost, making of 25
cottonstrainer bugs *40*
crickets *14*, *15*, *29*, *45*
crops, attacked by insects 48–0
cuticle 28
cyanide 31

D

damselflies *17*
danger, rapid reaction to 22
dark green fritillary *12*
deception 28
defence equipment 28–9
desert beetles *39*
desert climate 38
disease transmitters 49
diving beetle, oxygen for 37
Dorcadron scopoli beetle,
    flightless 16
dragonflies *10*, *17*, *36*, 36, 44
Dromius quadrimaculatus 13
dung beetles 34

E

earthworms 13
earwigs *11*, *12*, 12, *13*
egg shells, tough 39
eggs 43
    butterfly *45*
    in the desert 39
empid fly *17*
escape mechanism 16
Euptychia clio 25
eyes *14*, 14
    compound 22

F

feeding 24–5
feelers *14*, 14, 23
    and sense of smell 23
field cricket *13*
flag-legged bugs *41*
flea beetles *24*
fleas 13, *20*
flies 13
flight 16–19
    energy used 17
flight patterns 19
formic acid 30
foxgloves *35*
fungus gardens *32*

G

gall wasps *35*, 35
galls *35*, 35
gills 37
grasshoppers *11*, *15*, 20
    foam defence *31*
great diving beetle *36*
green brindled beauty *29*

H

hairs *34*
    of hopping insects 21
    poisonous 28
head *14*, 14
heath fritillary, protected *51*, 51
hibernation *45*
hindlegs 37
    for jumping 20
honey bees *14*, 14, *15*, *46*, 46
    colonies of 32
    communication 33–4
    using a sun compass 18
    wild bees' nests 34
honeycomb *46*
hoppers 20–1, 48, 49
hornet *46*
horse fly 22
house cricket *11*
house pests *13*, 13
house-flies *10*, 17, 22
hovering 16

I

Indian moon moth 25
insect body 14–15
insect groups *10*
insect habitats 11
insect homes 32–5
insect protection 28–31
insects 10–13
    can damage human life 49
    endangered species 50–1
    freshwater 36–7
    with gills 37
    harmful 48–9
    helpful 46–7
    winged 16–17
    wingless 16

J

jaws *15*, 15, 24–5
jet swimmers 36–7
jewel beetle *39*
jumping 20–1, 22

K

Kallima butterfly *29*

L

lacebug *11*
ladybirds
    eating aphids 27, 46, *47*
    as predators 47
lantern fly bugs *40*
larvae 25, 43
    butterfly *45*
    caddis fly *37*
    with gills 37
    mosquito *36*
leaf hoppers *21*
leaf insects *29*
leaf litter 12
leaf mimic bush cricket *29*
leaf mine 35
leaf-rolling weevil *40*
legs 15
    hindlegs 20, 37
life cycles
    butterflies 45, *45*
    dragonfly 44
    shield bugs 42, *42*
lifespan, adult insects 44
light seekers 19
limbs, jointed 10
locusts 20–1, *48, 48*, 49
longhorn beetles *14*
    protective wing case *18*
love dust 18
lycid beetle *28*

M

malaria *49*
maybugs *16, 19*
mayflies 36
meadow grasshopper 20
metamorphosis, complete and
    incomplete 42–5
migration *45 , 19*
mimicry *28*, 28, *29*, 30
mining bee, hairy-legged *34*
monarch butterfly *45 , 19*
monkey-hopper *51*

mosquitoes 13, 17, *49*
moths 13, *29*
    attracted by lights 19
    feeding 25
mouthparts *14*, 14, 15
    chewing *see* jaws
    piercing *24*, 24, 37
muscles, for wing beating 17, *17*

N

Namib Desert 38
natural habitats, disappearance
    of 50
nectar 33, 34
    into honey *46, 46*
night beetles *39*
nurseries 33
nymphs 36, 43

O

oil beetle *25*
    in the desert 38
Onymacris unguicularis 38
oxygen, dissolved in water 37

P

painted lady butterfly *10*
Palamedes swallowtail 45
parasitic wasps 47
Peruvian beetle *23*
Peruvian moth *28*
Phymateus morbillosus 31
piercing mouthparts 15, *24*, 24, 37
Pine chafer *13*
plant bugs *40*
playing dead 21, 22
poison *31*
    oil 25
pollen 33
pollination 46
pond skater *37, 37*
praying mantis *11*, 26–7, *27, 29*
    endangered in Madagascar *50*
predators 26–7
pupae 43, *45*
pussmoth caterpillar 30

R

rainforests
    destruction of *50, 50*
    insects in 40–1
red assassin bug *13*
reproduction, quick 10
resin 33
robberfly *16, 26*
Rose pin cushion 35
rosea bugs *31*
Rosechafer beetle *10*
rostrums *40*

S

saguaro cactus *38*
scales, colouring wings 18
scent detection *23, 23*
scent scales 18
Scorpion fly *10*
Searcher *13*
senses 22–3
Sepiodium tricuspidatum 39
Sexton beetle *13*
Shield bug *15*
silk thread *45*
silkworms 46, 47
silverfish *13*
skeletons, external 11, 28
skippers *41*
sleeping sickness 49
smell, sense of 22, 22–3
smelling holes 23
social insects 32–3
soldier termites *11*, 32
Southern hawker dragonfly *10*
spiders, injecting poison *31*
spines 28
    poisonous *31*
spiracles *14*
sponge mouthparts 15
springtails 12, *21*
stick insects *11*, *29*, 29
stink bugs 28–9
stomach 14
sun compass 19
sunbathing 33
sweet potato hawkmoth
    caterpillar *45*

T

teamwork, in colonies 33
termite mounds *32*
termites 32
    and fungus gardens 32
    tetrasticus galactopus 47
thorax *14*, 14, *17*
thorn bugs *30*
thrips *11*
Tiger beetle *15*
touch and feel sensations 22
tree trunks, recycling of 41
treehoppers *21*
tsetse fly 49

V

vespid wasp *15*
violet ground beetle *13*
vision 22

W

warning colour 16, 18, *20, 21*, 28,
    31, 39
wasps *15*, 33, 47
    nests 33
    as predators 47
water 33
    conservation in deserts 38
water boatman *37*, 37
weevils *40*
Whirligigs *37*
Wildlife and Countryside Act 51
wing case, fused *16*
wing-beat cycles 17
wings 15
    for advertisement or disguise
        18
    beating of *16, 17*, 17
    hinged *16*
wood ants *15*, 33
woodlice 13

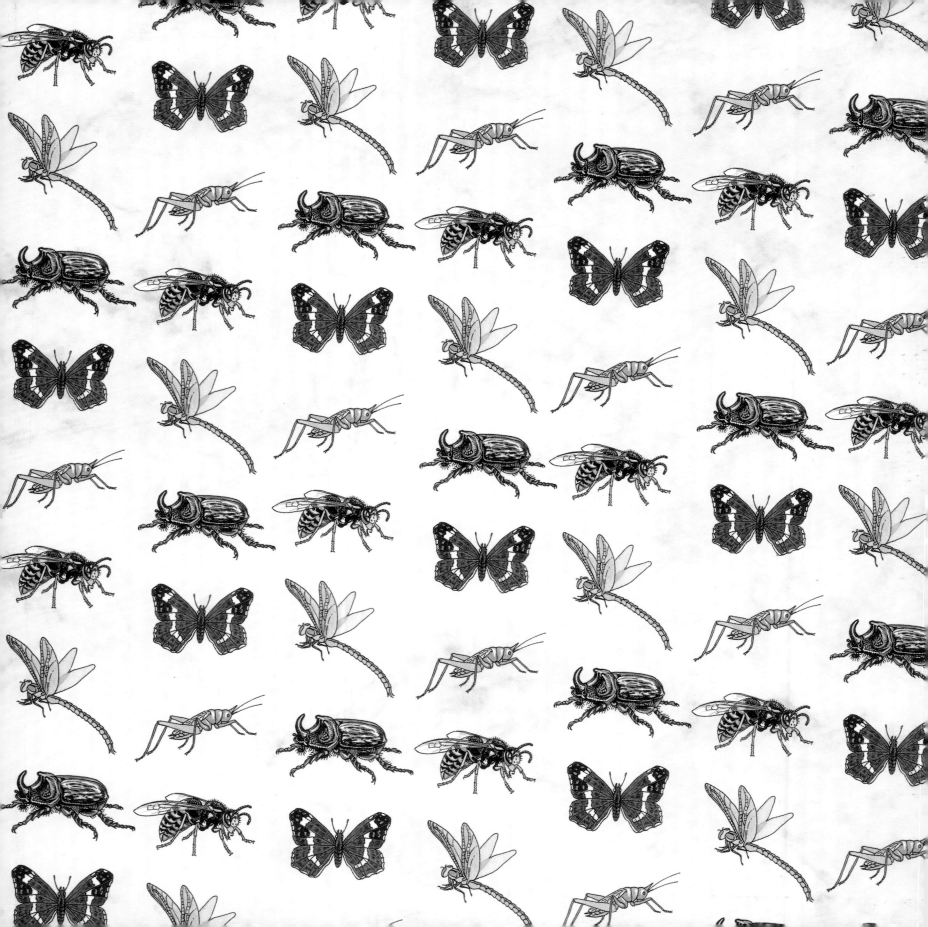